THE CONCISE GUIDE TO PATENTS TRADEMARKS AND COPYRIGHTS

THE
CONCISE
GUIDE TO **PATENTS**
TRADEMARKS
AND **COPYRIGHTS**

EDITED BY **SOLOMON J. SCHEPPS**

BELL PUBLISHING COMPANY
NEW YORK

Copyright © MCMLXXX by Crown Publishers, Inc.
All rights reserved.

This edition is published by Bell Publishing Company, a
division of Crown Publishers, Inc.
a b c d e f g h
BELL 1980 EDITION

Manufactured in the United States of America

Design by Ronald Dorfman.

Library of Congress Cataloging in Publication Data

Main entry under title:

The Concise guide to patents, trademarks, and copyrights.

   1. Patent laws and legislation—United States.
2. Copyright—United States. 3. Trade-marks—United
States. I. Schepps, Solomon J.
KF3095.C63   346.73'048   79-27353
ISBN 0-517-31003-1

Contents

Foreword

Every inventor, manufacturer, and artist wants to take full advantage of patent, trademark, and copyright laws, which are there to protect the ownership of his work. But he does not always know how to go about obtaining the legal protection he desires.

This book provides a thorough explanation of these laws, and outlines each step necessary to the securing of patent protection, as well as summarizing trademark and copyright laws and procedures. Questions such as these are answered:

Whom do I contact?

What do I have to do to apply?

How much does it cost?

How long does it take?

Exactly what protection do I get?

How long does this protection last?

In the case of patents, the government processes to determine eligibility and originality are explained in detail, and the applicant will find that these are largely intended to further protect ownership. Everything involved in application for protection, down to the size of paper to be submitted, is described. Among other matters discussed are infringement on ownership rights, transfer of ownership, and publications of the government offices that provide more highly technical or specialized information.

The copyright laws were drastically revised in 1978. This book shows how the new laws differ from the old, how they are better, and how to take advantage of them.

Patent, trademark, and copyright laws are complex, but they are by no means impenetrable. Armed with this book, any applicant for legal protection under these laws will find the application process comprehensible and straightforward.

SOLOMON J. SCHEPPS

PART
ONE **PATENTS**

Introduction

The reason for the legislation of patent laws is that an inventor has no common law right to monopolize his invention. The Constitution of the United States gives Congress the power to enact laws relating to patents, in Article 1, Section 8, which reads "Congress shall have power . . . to promote the progress of science and useful arts, by securing for limited times to authors and inventors the exclusive right to their respective writings and discoveries." Regarding patents, the word *useful* is of particular importance, for inventions of dubious usefulness would certainly not promote the progress of science.

In order for an invention to be patentable, it must be novel and nonobvious, as well as adding to the sum of useful knowledge. *Nonobvious* means that anyone with average knowledge and skills in the field should not be able to conceive of and create the invention with little effort, and that no prior art should directly imply it. The following things may be patented: processes (including new uses of old processes), machines, manufactured products, compositions of matter, improvements, asexually reproduced plants, and ornamental or decorative designs (even though they may exist by virtue of something outside themselves). Ideas, independent of any means to actualize them, are not patentable, nor are newly discovered laws of nature (in properly written form, these should be eligible for copyright).

A patent gives an inventor "the right to exclude others from making, using, or selling" his invention in this country. By *inventor* is meant the first inventor. If one invents something that has already been patented, even if he is entirely without knowledge of its prior invention, he may not obtain a patent for it. Furthermore, a patent can be withdrawn if it is shown that the owner of the patent stole his idea from someone else or that a prior art or invention clearly implies his invention.

Patents last for 17 years from the date of issuance, after which time the invention becomes public property. Ownership of patents can be transferred, but the period covered by the statute of limitations does not begin anew. Patents are not usually renewable.

The Patent Office is a public office that has complete records of all patented inventions. In addition, it publishes a weekly gazette containing information on all inventions patented that week.

Application for a patent and its subsequent securing is not difficult. It involves several steps, but the steps are clearly delineated. There is ample time between each step for the Patent Office and the applicant to insure that everything is correct and legitimate.

The following detailed explanation and practical description of patent laws should be read carefully by anyone seeking to patent an invention.

What Is a Patent?

A patent for an invention is a grant of certain rights by the government, acting through the Patent and Trademark Office, to an inventor.

The patent grant lasts for 17 years, and extends throughout the United States and its territories and possessions.

The right conferred by the patent grant is, in the language of the statute and of the grant itself, "the right to exclude others from making, using, or selling" the invention. What is granted is not the right to make, use, or sell, but the right to exclude others from making, using, or selling the invention.

Some persons occasionally confuse patents, copyrights, and trademarks. Although there may be some resemblance in the rights of these three kinds of intangible property, they are completely different and serve different purposes. The reader is referred to Parts II and III of this book for an explanation of trademarks and copyrights.

Patent Laws

The Constitution of the United States gives Congress the power to enact laws relating to patents, in Article 1, Section 8, which reads "Congress shall have power . . . to promote the progress of science and useful arts, by securing for limited times to authors and inventors the exclusive right to their respective writings and discoveries." Under power Congress has from time to time enacted various laws relating to patents: The first patent law was enacted in 1790. The law now in effect is a general revision which was enacted July 19, 1952, and which came into effect January 1, 1953. This law is reprinted in a pamphlet entitled *Patent Laws,* which is sold by the Superintendent of Documents, U.S. Government Printing Office, Washington, D.C. 20402.

The patent law specifies the subject matter for which a patent may be obtained and the conditions for patentability. The law establishes the Patent and Trademark Office for administering the law relating to the granting of patents, and contains various other provisions relating to patents.

What Can Be Patented

The patent law specifies the general field of subject matter that can be patented and the conditions under which a patent may be obtained.

In the language of the statute, any person who "invents or discovers any new and useful process, machine, manufacture, or composition of matter, or any new and useful improvements therefore, may obtain a patent," subject to the conditions and requirements of the law. By the word "process" is meant a process or method, and new processes, primarily industrial or technical processes, may be patented. The term "machine" used in the statute needs no explanation. The term "manufacture" refers to all articles that are made. The term "composition of matter" refers to chemical compositions and may include mixtures of ingredients as well as new chemical compounds. These classes of subject matter taken together include practically everything made by man and the processes for making them.

The Atomic Energy Act of 1954 excludes the patenting of inventions useful solely in the utilization of special nuclear material or atomic energy for atomic weapons.

The statute specifies that the subject matter must be "useful," that is, it must serve a useful function. A machine that will not operate to perform its intended purpose, for example, would not be called useful. Alleged inventions of perpetual motion machines are refused patents.

Interpretations of the statute by the courts have defined the limits of the field of subject matter that can be patented. Thus it has been held that methods of doing business and printed matter cannot be patented.

In the case of mixtures of ingredients, such as medicines, a patent cannot be granted unless there is more to the mixture than the effect of its components. (So-called patent medicines are ordinarily not patented; the phrase "patent medicine" in this connection does not mean that the medicine is patented.) It is often said that a patent cannot be obtained for a mere idea or suggestion. The patent is granted for the new machine, manufacture, etc., as has been said, and not for the idea or suggestion of the new machine. As will be stated later, a complete description of the actual machine or other subject matter sought to be patented is required.

Novelty and Other Conditions for Obtaining a Patent

In order for an invention to be patentable it must be new as defined in the statute.

If the invention has been described in a printed publication anywhere in the world, or if it has been in public use or on sale in this country before the date that the applicant made his invention, a patent cannot be obtained. If the invention has been described in a printed publication anywhere, or has been in public use or on sale in this country more than one year before the date on which an application for patent is filed in this country, a valid patent cannot be obtained. In this connection it is immaterial when the invention was made, or whether the printed publication or public use was by the inventor himself or by someone else. If the inventor describes the invention in a printed publication or uses the invention publicly, or places it on sale, he must apply for a patent before one year has gone by, otherwise any right to a patent will be lost.

Even if the subject matter sought to be patented is not exactly shown by the prior art, and involves one or more differences over the most nearly similar thing already known, a patent may still be refused if the differences would be obvious. The subject matter sought to be patented must be sufficiently different from what has been used or described before. For example, the substitution of one material for another, or changes in size, are ordinarily not patentable.

The United States Patent and Trademark Office

Congress has established the United States Patent and Trademark Office to perform the function of issuing patents on behalf of the government. The Patent and Trademark Office as a distinct bureau dates from the year 1802 when a separate official in the Department of State who became known as "Superintendent of Patents" was placed in charge of patents. The revision of the patent laws enacted in 1836 reorganized the Patent and Trademark Office and designated the official in charge as Commissioner of Patents and Trademarks. The Patent and Trademark Office remained in the Department of State until 1849 when it was transferred to the Department of the Interior and in 1925 it was transferred to the Department of Commerce, in which Department it is today.

The chief functions of the Patent and Trademark Office are to administer the patent laws as they relate to the granting of letters patent for inventions, and to perform other duties relating to patents. It examines applications for patents to ascertain if the applicants are entitled to patents under the law, and grants the patents when they are so entitled; it publishes issued patents and various publications concerning patents and patent laws, records assignments of patents, maintains a search room for the use of the public to examine issued patents and records, supplies copies of records and other papers, and the like. Analogous and similar functions are performed with respect to the registration of trademarks. The Patent and Trademark Office has no jurisdiction over questions of infringement and the enforcement of patents, nor over matters relating to the promotion or utilization of patents or inventions.

The head of the Office is the Commissioner of Patents and Trademarks and his staff includes several assistant commissioners of patents and other officials. As head of the Office, the Commissioner supervises or performs all duties with respect to the granting and using of patents and the registration of trademarks; exercises general supervision over the entire work of the Patent and Trademark Office; prescribes the rules, subject to the approval of the Secretary of Commerce, for the conduct of proceedings in the Patent and Trademark Office and for recognition of attorneys and agents; decides various questions brought before him by petition as prescribed by the rules, and performs other duties necessary and required for the administration of the Patent and Trademark Office and the performance of its function.

The examination of applications for patents is the largest and most important function of the Patent and Trademark Office. The work is divided among a number of examining groups, each group having jurisdiction over certain assigned fields of invention. Each group is headed by a group director and staffed by a number of examiners. The examiners perform the work of examining applications for patents and determine whether patents can be granted. An appeal can be taken to the Board of Appeals from their decisions refusing patents, and a review by the Commissioner of Patents and Trademarks may be had on other matters by petition. The examiners also determine when an "interference" (see p. 50) exists between pending applications or between a pending application and a patent, institute interference proceedings in such cases, and hear and decide certain preliminary questions raised by contestants.

In addition to the examining groups, the Patent and Trademark Office has a number of sections, divisions, and branches that perform various other services, such as receiving and distributing mail, receiving new applications, handling sales of printed copies of patents, making copies of records, inspecting drawings, recording assignments, and so on.

At the present time the Patent and Trademark Office has about 2,700 employees, about half of whom are examiners and others with technical and legal training. Patent applications are received at the rate of over 90,000 per year. The Patent and Trademark Office receives over three million pieces of mail each year.

PUBLICATIONS OF THE PATENT AND TRADEMARK OFFICE

Patents. The specification and accompanying drawings of all patents are published on the day they are granted, and printed copies are sold to the public by the Patent and Trademark Office. Over 4 million patents have been issued.

Printed copies of any patent identified by its patent number may be purchased from the Patent and Trademark Office at a cost of 50 cents each, postage free, except plant patents, which are $1.00 each, and design patents, which are 20 cents each.

Future patents classified in subclasses containing subject matter of interest may be obtained, as they issue, by prepayment of a deposit and a service charge. For the cost of such subscription service, a separate inquiry should be sent to the Patent and Trademark Office.

Official Gazette of the United States Patent and Trademark Office. The *Official Gazette* of the United States Patent and Trademark Office is the official journal relating to patents and trademarks. It has been published weekly since January 1872 (replacing the old "Patent Office Reports"), and is now issued each Tuesday, simultaneously with the weekly issue of the patents. It contains a claim and a selected figure of the drawings of each patent granted on that day; notices of patent and trademark suits; indexes of patents and patentees; list of patents available for license or sale; and much general information such as orders, notices, changes in rules, changes in classification, etc. The *Official Gazette* is sold on subscription and by single copies by the Superintendent of Documents, U.S. Government Printing Office, Washington, D.C. 20402.

Since July, 1952, the illustrations and claims of the patents have been arranged in the *Official Gazette* according to the Patent and Trademark Office classification of subject matter, permitting ready reference to patents in any particular field. Street addresses of patentees have been published since May 24, 1960, and a geographical index of residences of inventors has been included since May 18, 1965. Copies of the *Official Gazette* may be found in public libraries of larger cities.

Index of Patents. This annual index to the *Official Gazette* is currently in two volumes, one an index of patentees and the other an index by subject matter of the patents. Sold by Superintendent of Documents.

Index of Trademarks. An annual index of registrants of trademarks. Sold by Superintendent of Documents.

Manual of Classification. A looseleaf book containing a list of all the classes and subclasses of inventions in the Patent and Trademark Office classification systems, a subject matter index, and other information relating to classification. Substitute pages are issued from time to time. Annual subscription includes the basic manual and substitute pages. Sold by Superintendent of Documents.

Classification Definitions. Contains the changes in classification of patents as well as definitions of new and revised classes and subclasses. Sold by Patent and Trademark Office.

Weekly Class Sheets. Lists showing classification of each patent in the weekly issue of the *Official Gazette.* Sold on annual subscription by Patent and Trademark Office.

Patent Laws. A compilation of patent laws in force. Sold by Superintendent of Documents.

Title 37 Code of Federal Regulations. Includes Rules of Practice for Patents, Trademarks and Copyrights. Available from the Superintendent of Documents.

Trademark Rules of Practice of the Patent and Trademark Office With Forms and Statutes. Rules governing the procedures in the Patent and Trademark Office in trademark matters and a compilation of trademark laws in force. Sold by Superintendent of Documents.

General Information Concerning Trademarks. A description of trademark law and how to obtain a trademark. Copies may be purchased from Superintendent of Documents.

Patents and Inventions—An Information Aid for Inventors. Provides information which may help inventors decide whether to apply for patents and aids them in obtaining patent protection and promoting their inventions. Sold by Superintendent of Documents.

Directory of Registered Patent Attorneys and Agents Arranged by States and Countries. A geographical listing of patent attorneys and agents registered to practice before the U.S. Patent and Trademark Office. Sold by Superintendent of Documents.

Manual of Patent Examining Procedure. A looseleaf manual which serves primarily as a detailed reference work on patent examining practice and procedure for the Patent and Trademark Office's Examining Corps. Subscription service includes basic manual, quarterly revisions, and change notices. Sold by Superintendent of Documents.

Guide for Patent Draftsmen. Patent and Trademark Office requirements for patent drawings. Illustrated. Sold by Superintendent of Documents.

The Story of the United States Patent Office. A chronological account of the development of the U.S. Patent and Trademark Office and patent system and of inventions which have had unusual impact on the American economy and society. Sold by Superintendent of Documents.

Patent Cooperation Treaty. Copy of the Treaty Articles and Regulations available in limited quantities from Patent and Trademark Office.

GENERAL INFORMATION AND CORRESPONDENCE

All business with the Patent and Trademark Office should be transacted in writing. The personal attendance of applicants at the Office is unnecessary. Mail should be addressed to *"COMMISSIONER OF PATENTS AND TRADEMARKS, WASHINGTON, D.C. 20231."* The Office is located at Crystal Plaza, 2021 Jefferson Davis Highway, Arlington, Va.

Applicants and attorneys are required to conduct their business with the Office with decorum and courtesy. Papers presented in violation of this requirement will be returned.

A separate letter (but not necessarily in a separate envelope) should be written in relation to each distinct subject of inquiry, such as assignments for recording, payment of issue fees, orders for printed copies of patents, order for photographic copies of records, and requests for other services. None of these should be included with letters responding to Office actions in applications.

When a letter concerns a patent, it should state the

name of the patentee, the invention, and the patent number and date.

In making inquiry concerning the status of his application, the inventor should be sure to give its serial number and filing date and the Group Art unit number.

The zip code should be included as part of the address in all correspondence.

An order for a copy of an assignment must give the book and page or reel and frame of the record, as well as the name of the inventor; otherwise, an additional charge is made for the time consumed in making a search for the assignment.

Applications for patents are not open to the public, and no information concerning them is released except on written authority of the applicant, his assignee, or his attorney, or when necessary to the conduct of the business of the Office. Patents and related records, including records of any decisions, the records of assignments other than those relating to assignments of patent applications, books, and other records and papers in the Office are open to the public. They may be inspected in the Patent and Trademark Office Search Room, or copies may be ordered.

The Office cannot respond to inquiries concerning the novelty and patentability of an invention in advance of the filing of application, give advice as to possible infringement of a patent, advise of the propriety of filing an application, respond to inquiries as to whether or to whom any alleged invention has been patented, or act as an expounder of the patent law or as counselor for individuals, except in deciding questions arising before it in regularly filed cases.

Information of a general nature may be furnished either directly or by supplying or calling attention to an appropriate publication.

LIBRARY, SEARCH ROOM SEARCHES

The Scientific Library of the Patent and Trademark Office at Crystal Plaza, 2021 Jefferson Davis Highway, Arlington, Va., has available for public use over 120,000 volumes of scientific and technical books in various languages, about 90,000 bound volumes of periodicals devoted to science and technology, the official journals of foreign patent offices, and over 8 million foreign patents in bound volumes. (In many cases there are two sets of foreign patents, one set arranged in numerical order and another set arranged according to the subject classification system of the country of origin of the patents.)

A Search Room is provided where the public may search and examine United States patents granted since 1836. Patents are arranged according to the Patent and Trademark Office classification system of over 300 subject classes and 64,000 subclasses. By searching in these classified patents, it is possible to determine, before actually filing an application, whether an invention has been anticipated by a United States patent, and it is also possible to obtain the information contained in patents relating to any field of endeavor. The Search Room contains a set of United States patents arranged in numerical order and a complete set of the *Official Gazette*.

A Record Room also is maintained where the public may inspect the records and files of issued patents and other open records.

Applicants and their attorneys or agents may examine their own cases in the Record Room, and public records may be examined in the Scientific Library, Search Room, or Record Room, as the case may be. Applicants, their attorneys or agents, and the general public are not entitled to use the records and files in the examiners' rooms.

The Search Room is open from 8 a.m. to 8 p.m. Monday through Friday except on legal holidays.

Since a patent is not always granted when an application is filed, many inventors attempt to make their own investigation before applying for a patent. This may be done in the Search Room of the Patent and Trademark Office, and to a limited extent in some public libraries. Patent attorneys or agents may be employed to make a so-called preliminary search through the prior United States patents to discover if the particular device or one similar to it has been shown in some prior patent. This search is not always as complete as that made by the Patent and Trademark Office during the examination of an application, but only serves, as its name indicates, a preliminary purpose. For this reason, the Patent and Trademark Office examiner may, and often does, reject claims in an application on the basis of prior patents or publications not found in the preliminary search.

Those who cannot come to the Search Room may order from the Patent and Trademark Office copies of lists of original patents or of cross-referenced patents contained in the subclasses comprising the field of search, and inspect printed copies of the patents in a library which has a numerically arranged set of patents. These libraries and their locations are:

CALIFORNIA	*Los Angeles:* Los Angeles Public Library; *Sunnyvale:* Public Library[1]
GEORGIA	*Atlanta:* Georgia Tech Library
ILLINOIS	*Chicago:* Public Library
MASSACHUSETTS	*Boston:* Public Library
MICHIGAN	*Detroit:* Public Library
MISSOURI	*Kansas City:* Linda Hall Library; *St. Louis:* Public Library
NEW JERSEY	*Newark:* Public Library
NEW YORK	*Albany:* Library of the University of the State of New York; *Buffalo:* Buffalo and Erie County Public Library; *New York:* Public Library
OHIO	*Cincinnati:* Public Library; *Cleveland:* Public Library; *Columbus:* Ohio State University Library; *Toledo:* Public Library

[1]Arranged by subject matter, collection dates from Jan. 2, 1962.

OKLAHOMA *Stillwater:* Oklahoma A&M College Library

PENNSYLVANIA *Philadelphia:* Franklin Institute; *Pittsburgh:* Carnegie Library

RHODE ISLAND *Providence:* Public Library

WISCONSIN *Madison:* State Historical Society of Wisconsin Library; *Milwaukee:* Public Library

The Patent and Trademark Office has also prepared on microfilm lists of the numbers of the patents issued in each of its subclasses, and many libraries have purchased copies of these lists. In libraries which have the lists and a copy of the Manual of Classification, and also a set of patent copies or the *Official Gazette,* it is unnecessary for the searcher to communicate with the Patent and Trademark Office before commencing his search, as he can learn from the Manual of Classification the subclasses which his search should include, then identify the number of the patents in these subclasses from the microfilm lists, and examine the patent copies so identified, or the disclosures of these patents in the *Official Gazette* volumes.

While the classification printed on any patent is correct at the time the patent is issued, it should be noted that the constantly expanding body of patents often requires reclassification. As a result, the classification indicated on the patent may be incorrect at a later date.

Attorneys and Agents

The preparation of an application for patent and the conducting of the proceedings in the Patent and Trademark Office to obtain the patent is an undertaking requiring knowledge of patent law and Patent and Trademark Office practice as well as knowledge of the scientific or technical matters involved in the particular invention.

The inventor may prepare his own application and file it in the Patent and Trademark Office and conduct the proceedings himself, but unless he is familiar with these matters or studies them in detail, he may get into considerable difficulty. While a patent may be obtained in many cases by persons not skilled in this work, there would be no assurance that the patent obtained would adequately protect the particular invention.

Most inventors employ the services of persons known as patent attorneys or patent agents. The statute gives the Patent and Trademark Office the power to make rules and regulations governing the recognition of patent attorneys and agents to practice before the Patent and Trademark Office, and persons who are not recognized by the Patent and Trademark Office for this practice are not permitted by law to represent inventors. The Patent and Trademark Office maintains a register of attorneys and agents. To be admitted to this register, a person must comply with the regulations prescribed by the Office, which now require a showing that the person is of good moral character and of good repute and that he has the legal and scientific and technical qualifications necessary to enable him to render applicants for patents valuable service. Certain of these qualifications must be demonstrated by the passing of an examination. Those admitted to the examination must have a college degree in engineering or science or the equivalent of such a degree. The Patent and Trademark Office registers both attorneys at law and persons who are not attorneys at law. The former persons are now referred to as "patent attorneys" and the latter persons are referred to as "patent agents." Insofar as the work of preparing an application for patent and conducting the prosecution in the Patent and Trademark Office is concerned, patent agents are usually just as well-qualified as patent attorneys, although patent agents cannot conduct patent litigation in the courts or perform various services which the local jurisdiction considers as practicing law. For example, a patent agent could not draw up a contract relating to a patent, such as an assignment or a license, if the state in which he resides considers drawing contracts as practicing law.

By regulation, registered patent attorneys and agents are forbidden to advertise for patent business. Some individuals and organizations that are not registered advertise their services in the fields of patent searching and patent promotions. Such individuals and organizations cannot represent inventors before the Patent and Trademark Office. They are not subject to Patent and Trademark Office discipline, and the Office cannot assist inventors in dealing with them.

The Patent and Trademark Office cannot recommend any particular attorney or agent, or aid in the selection of an attorney or agent, as by stating in response to inquiry that a named patent attorney, agent, or firm, is "reliable" or "capable." The Patent and Trademark Office publishes a Directory of all registered patent attorneys and agents who have indicated their availability to accept new clients, arranged by states, cities, and foreign countries.

The telephone directories of most large cities have, in the classified section, a heading for patent attorneys under which those in that area are listed. Many large cities have associations of patent attorneys.

In employing a patent attorney or agent, the inventor executes a power of attorney or authorization of agent, which must be filed in the Patent and Trademark Office and is usually a part of the application papers. When an attorney has been appointed, the Office does not communicate with the inventor directly but conducts the correspondence with the attorney since he is acting for the inventor thereafter, although the inventor is free to contact the Patent and Trademark Office concerning the status of his application. The inventor may remove the attorney or agent by revoking the power of authorization. See form 8, page 95.

The Patent and Trademark Office has the power to disbar, or suspend from practicing before it, persons guilty of gross misconduct, but this can be done only after a full hearing with the presentation of evidence concerning the misconduct. The Patent and Trademark Office will receive and, in appropriate cases, act upon complaints against attorneys and agents. The fees charged to inventors by patent attorneys and agents for their professional services are not subject to regulation by the Patent and Trademark Office. Definite evidence of overcharging may afford basis for Patent and Trademark Office action, but the Office rarely intervenes in disputes concerning fees.

Who May Apply for a Patent

According to the statute, only the inventor may apply for a patent, with certain exceptions. If a person who is not the inventor should apply for a patent, the patent, if it were obtained, would be void. The person applying in such a case who falsely states that he is the inventor would also be subject to criminal penalties. If the inventor is dead, the application may be made by his legal representatives, that is, the administrator or executor of his estate, in his place. If the inventor is insane, the application for patent may be made by his guardian, in his place. If an inventor refuses to apply for a patent or cannot be found, a joint inventor or a person having a proprietary interest in the invention may apply on behalf of the missing inventor.

If two or more persons make an invention jointly, they apply for a patent as joint inventors. A person who makes a financial contribution is not a joint inventor and cannot be joined in the application as an inventor. It is possible to correct an innocent mistake in omitting a joint inventor or in erroneously joining a person as an inventor.

Officers and employees of the Patent and Trademark Office are prohibited by law from applying for a patent or acquiring, directly or indirectly, except by inheritance or bequest, any patent or any right or interest in any patent.

Application for Patent

The application for patent is made to the Commissioner of Patents and Trademarks and includes:

(1) A written document that comprises a specifica-

tion (description and claims), and an oath or declaration;

(2) A drawing in those cases in which a drawing is possible; and

(3) The filing fee.

The specification and oath or declaration must be in English and must be legibly written or printed in permanent ink on one side of the paper. The Office prefers typewriting on legal size paper, 8 to $8\frac{1}{2}$ by $10\frac{1}{2}$ to 13 inches, $1\frac{1}{2}$ or double spaced, with margins of 1 inch on the left-hand side and at the top. If the papers filed are not correctly, legibly, and clearly written, the Patent and Trademark Office may require typewritten or printed papers instead.

The application for patent is not accepted and placed in the files for examination until all its required parts, complying with the rules relating thereto, are received. (Sometimes, however, certain minor informalities are waived subject to correction when required.)

If the papers and parts are incomplete, or so defective that they cannot be accepted as a complete application for examination, the applicant will be notified; the papers will be held for six months for completion and, if not completed by then, will be returned or otherwise disposed of. The filing fee may be refunded when an application is refused acceptance because it is incomplete.

All parts of the complete application should be deposited in the Office together; otherwise, each part must be signed separately, accompanied by a letter accurately and clearly connecting it with the other parts of the application.

All applications are numbered in regular order, and the applicant is informed of the serial number and filing date of the complete application by filing receipt. The filing date of the application is the date on which a complete and acceptable application is received in the Patent and Trademark Office, or the date on which the last part completing such application is received in the case of a previously incomplete or defective application.

OATH OR DECLARATION, SIGNATURE

The oath or declaration of the applicant is required by statute. The inventor must make an oath or declaration stating that he believes himself to be the original and first inventor of the subject matter of the application, and he must make various other allegations required by the statute and by the Patent and Trademark Office rules. The oath must be sworn to by the inventor before a notary public or other officer authorized to administer oaths. A declaration may be used in lieu of an oath as part of the original application for a patent involving designs, plants, and other patentable inventions; for reissue patents; when claiming matter originally shown or described but not originally claimed; or when filing a divisional or continuing application. Sample forms for oaths and declarations may be found beginning on p. 81 of this book. Illustrative declaration forms for other uses may be found in Title 37 of the Code of Federal Regulations.

The application must be signed by the inventor in person, or by the person entitled by law to make application on the inventor's behalf. A full first or middle name of each inventor without abbreviation and a middle or first initial, if any, is required. The post-office address of the inventor is also required.

The papers in a complete application will not be returned for any purpose whatever, nor will the filing fee be returned. If applicants have not preserved copies of the papers, the Office will furnish copies at the usual cost.

FILING FEES

The filing fee of an application for an original patent, except in design cases, consists of a basic fee and additional fees. The basic fee is $65 and entitles the applicant to present 10 claims, including not more than 1 in independent form. An additional fee of $10 is required for each claim in independent form which is in excess of 1 and an additional fee of $2 is required for each claim (whether independent or dependent) which is in excess of a total of 10 claims.

The following formula may be used in the calculation of the filing fee:

```
Basic Fee .............................. $65.00
Additional Fees:
   Total number of claims
      in excess of 10, times $2 ............. _____
   Number of independent claims
      in excess of 1, times $10 ............. _____
   Total Filing Fee ..................... _____
```

To avoid errors in the payment of fees it is suggested that a table such as given above be included in the letter of transmittal.

In calculating fees, a claim is in dependent form if it incorporates by reference a single preceding claim, which may be an independent or a dependent claim, and includes all the limitations of the claim incorporated by reference.

The law also provides for the payment of additional fees on presentation of claims after the application is filed.

When an amendment is filed which presents additional claims over the total number already paid for, or additional independent claims over the number of independent claims already accounted for, it must be accompanied by an additional fees due.

SPECIFICATION (DESCRIPTION AND CLAIMS)

The specification must include a written description of the invention and of the manner and process of making and using it, and is required to be in such full, clear, concise, and exact terms that any person skilled in the art to which the invention pertains, or with which it is most nearly connected, can make and use the same.

The specifications must set forth the precise invention for which a patent is solicited, in such manner as to distinguish it from other inventions and from what is old. It must describe completely a specific embodiment of the process, machines, manufacture, composition of matter or improvements invented, and must explain the mode of operation or principle whenever applicable. The best mode contemplated by the inventor of carrying out his invention must be set forth.

In the case of an improvement, the specifications must particularly point out the part or parts of the process, machine, manufacture, or composition of matter to which the improvement relates, and the description should be confined to the specific improvement and to such parts as necessarily cooperate with it or as may be necessary to a complete understanding or description of it.

The title of the invention, which should be as short and specific as possible, should appear as a heading on the first page of the specification, if it does not otherwise appear at the beginning of the application.

A brief abstract of the technical disclosure in the specification must be set forth in a separate page immediately following the claims in a separate paragraph under the heading "Abstract of the Disclosure."

A brief summary of the invention indicating its nature and substance, which may include a statement of the object of the invention, commensurate with the invention as claimed and any object recited, should precede the detailed description. Such summary should be that of the invention as claimed.

When there are drawings, there should be a brief description of the several views of the drawings, and the detailed description of the invention should refer to the different views by specifying the numbers of the figures, and to the different parts by use of reference letters or numerals (preferably the latter).

The specification must conclude with one or more claims distinctly pointing out and claiming the subject matter which the applicant regards as his invention.

When more than one claim is presented, they may be placed in dependent form, meaning that a claim may refer back to and further restrict a single preceding claim.

The claim or claims must conform to the invention as set forth in the remainder of the specification, and the terms and phrases used in the claims must find clear support or antecedent basis in the description so that the meaning of the terms in the claims may be ascertainable by reference to the description.

The claims are brief descriptions of the subject matter of the invention, eliminating unnecessary details and reciting all essential features necessary to distinguish the invention from what is old. The claims are the operative part of the patent. Novelty and patentability are judged by the claims, and, when a patent is granted, questions of infringement are judged by the courts on the basis of the claims.

The following order of arrangement should be observed in framing the specification:

(a) Title of the invention; or a preamble stating the name, citizenship, and residence of the applicant and the title of the invention may be used.

(b) Cross-references to related applications, if any.

(c) Brief summary of the invention.

(d) Brief description of the several views of the drawing, if there are drawings.

(e) Detailed description.
(f) Claim or claims.
(g) Abstract of the disclosure.

DRAWING

The applicant for a patent will usually be required by statute to furnish a drawing of his invention whenever the nature of the case admits of it; this drawing must be filed with the application. This includes practically all inventions except compositions of matter or processes (although a drawing may be useful in the case of many processes).

The drawing must show every feature of the invention specified in the claims and is required by the Office rules to be in a particular form. The Office specifies the size of the sheet on which the drawing is made, the type of paper, the margins, and other details relating to the making of the drawing. The reason for specifying the standards in detail is that the drawings are printed and published in a uniform style when the patent issues, and the drawings must also be such that they can be readily understood by persons using the patent descriptions.

No names or other identification are permitted within the "sight" of the drawing, and applicants are expected to use the space above and between the hole locations to identify each sheet of drawings. This identification may consist of the attorney's name and docket number or the inventor's name and case number and may include the sheet number and the total number of sheets filed (for example, "sheet 2 of 4").

The following rules relate to the standards for drawings:

1.84 *Standards for drawings.*

(*a*) *Paper and ink.* Drawings must be made upon paper which is flexible, strong, white, smooth, non-shiny and durable. Two-ply or three-ply bristol board is preferred. The surface of the paper should be calendered and of a quality which will permit erasure and correction with India ink. India ink, or its equivalent in quality, is preferred for pen drawings to secure perfectly black solid lines. The use of white pigment to cover lines is not normally acceptable.

(*b*) *Size of sheet and margins.* The size of the sheets on which drawings are made may either be exactly $8\frac{1}{2}$ by 14 inches (21.6 by 35.6 cm.) or exactly 21.0 by 29.7 cm. (DIN size A4). All drawing sheets in a particular application must be the same size. One of the shorter sides of the sheet is regarded as its top. (1) On $8\frac{1}{2}$ by 14 inch drawing sheets, the drawing must include a top margin of 2 inches (5.1 cm.) and bottom and side margins of $\frac{1}{4}$ inch (6.4 mm.) from the edges, thereby leaving a "sight" precisely 8 by $11\frac{3}{4}$ inches (20.3 by 29.8 cm.). Margin border lines are not permitted. All work must be included within the "sight." The sheets may be provided with two $\frac{1}{4}$ inch (6.4 mm.) diameter holes having their center-lines spaced $\frac{11}{16}$ inch (17.5 mm.) below the top edge and $2\frac{3}{4}$ inches (7.0 cm.) apart, said holes being equally spaced from the respective side edges. (2) On 21.0 by 29.7 cm. drawing sheets, the drawing must include a top margin of at least 2.5 cm., a left side margin of 2.5 cm., a right side margin of 1.5 cm., and a bottom margin of 1.0 cm. Margin border lines are not permitted. All work must be contained within a sight size not to exceed 17 by 26.2 cm.

(c) *Character of lines.* All drawings must be made with drafting instruments or by a process which will give them satisfactory reproduction characteristics. Every line and letter must be durable, black, sufficiently dense and dark, uniformly thick and well defined; the weight of all lines and letters must be heavy enough to permit adequate reproduction. This direction applies to all lines however fine, to shading, and to lines representing cut surfaces in sectional views. All lines must be clean, sharp, and solid. Fine or crowded lines should be avoided. Solid black should not be used for sectional or surface shading. Freehand work should be avoided wherever it is possible to do so.

(d) *Hatching and shading.* (1) Hatching should be made by oblique parallel lines spaced sufficiently apart to enable the lines to be distinguished without difficulty. (2) Heavy lines on the shade side of objects should preferably be used except where they tend to thicken the work and obscure reference characters. The light should come from the upper left-hand corner at an angle of 45°. Surface delineations should preferably be shown by proper shading, which should be open.

(e) *Scale.* The scale to which a drawing is made ought to be large enough to show the mechanism without crowding when the drawing is reduced in size to two-thirds in reproduction, and views of portions of the mechanism on a larger scale should be used when necessary to show details clearly; two or more sheets should be used if one does not give sufficient room to accomplish this end, but the number of sheets should not be more than is necessary.

(f) *Reference characters.* The different views should

be consecutively numbered figures. Reference numerals (and letters, but numerals are preferred) must be plain, legible, and carefully formed, and not be encircled. They should, if possible, measure at least one-eighth of an inch (3.2 mm.) in height so that they may bear reduction to one twenty-fourth of an inch (1.1 mm.); and they may be slightly larger when there is sufficient room. They should not be so placed in the close and complex parts of the drawing as to interfere with a thorough comprehension of the same, and therefore should rarely cross or mingle with the lines. When necessarily grouped around a certain part, they should be placed at a little distance, at the closest point where there is available space, and connected by lines with the parts to which they refer. They should not be placed upon hatched or shaded surfaces but when necessary, a blank space may be left in the hatching or shading where the character occurs so that it shall appear perfectly distinct and separate from the work. The same part of an invention appearing in more than one view of the drawing must always be designated by the same character, and the same character must never be used to designate different parts. Reference signs not mentioned in the description shall appear in the drawing, and vice versa.

(*g*)* *Symbols, Legends.* Graphical drawing symbols and other labeled representations may be used for conventional elements when appropriate, subject to approval by the Office. The elements for which such symbols and labeled representations are used must be adequately identified in the specification. While descriptive matter on drawings is not permitted, suit-

---

*There is no section (h) in the procedures officially published by the Patent and Trademark Office.

able legends may be used, or may be required in proper cases, as in diagrammatic views and flow sheets or to show materials or where labeled representations are employed to illustrate conventional elements. Arrows may be required in proper cases, to show direction of movement. The lettering should be as large as, or larger than, the reference characters.

(*i*) *Views.* The drawings must contain as many figures as may be necessary to show the invention; the figures should be consecutively numbered, if possible in the order in which they appear. The figures may be plain, elevation, section, or perspective views, and detail views of portions of elements, on a larger scale if necessary, may also be used. Exploded views, with the separated parts of the same figure embraced by a bracket to show the relationship or order of assembly of various parts, are permissible. When necessary, a view of a large machine or device in its entirety may be broken and extended over several sheets if there is no loss in facility of understanding the view. Where figures on two or more sheets form in effect a single complete figure, the figures on the several sheets should be so arranged that the complete figure can be understood by laying the drawing sheets adjacent to one another. The arrangement should be such that no part of any of the figures appearing on the various sheets are concealed and that the complete figure can be understood even though spaces will occur in the complete figure because of the margins on the drawing sheets. The plane upon which a sectional view is taken should be indicated on the general view by a broken line, the ends of which should be designated by numerals corresponding to the figure number of the sectional view and have arrows applied to indicate the direction in which the view is taken. A moved position may be shown by a broken line superimposed upon a suitable figure if this can be done without crowding, otherwise a separate figure must be used for this purpose. Modified forms of construction can only be shown in separate figures. Views should not be connected by projection lines nor should center lines be used.

(j) *Arrangements of views.* All views on the same sheet should stand in the same direction and, if possible, stand so that they can be read with the sheet held in an upright position. If views longer than the width of the sheet are necessary for the clearest illustration of the invention, the sheet may be turned on its side so that the top of the sheet with the appropriate top margin is on the right-hand side. One figure must not be placed upon another or within the outline of another.

(k) *Figure for Official Gazette.* The drawing should, as far as possible, be so planned that one of the views will be suitable for publication in the Official Gazette as the illustration of the invention.

(l) *Extraneous matter.* Identifying indicia (such as the attorney's docket number, inventor's name, number of sheets, etc.) not to exceed $2\frac{3}{4}$ inches (7.0 cm.) in width may be placed in a centered location between the side edges within three-fourths inch (19.1 mm.) of the top edge. Authorized security markings may be placed on the drawings provided they are outside the illustrations and are removed when the material is declassified. Other extraneous matter will not be permitted upon the face of the drawing.

(m) *Transmission of drawings.* Drawings transmitted to the Office should be sent flat, protected by a sheet of heavy binder's board, or may be rolled for transmission in a suitable mailing tube, but must never be folded. If received creased or mutilated, new drawings will be required. (See rule 1.152 for design drawings, 1.165 for plant drawings, and 1.174 for reissue drawings.)

The requirements relating to drawings are strictly enforced, but a drawing not complying with all of the regulations is accepted for purpose of examination, and correction or a new drawing will be required later.

Applicants are advised to employ competent draftsmen to make their drawings. The Office may furnish drawings at the applicant's expense as promptly as its draftsmen can make them for applicants who cannot otherwise conveniently procure them.

MODELS, EXHIBITS, SPECIMENS

Models were once required as a part of the application when appropriate, and these models became a part of the record of the patent. Such models are no longer generally required since the description of the invention in the specification, and the drawings, must be sufficiently full and complete, and capable of being understood, to disclose the invention without the aid of a model. Now, a model will not be admitted unless specifically called for.

A model, working model, or other physical exhibit may be required by the Office if deemed necessary for any purpose on examination of the application. This is not done very often.

When the invention relates to a composition of matter, the applicant may be required to furnish specimens of the composition, or of its ingredients or intermediates, for inspection or experiment.

Examination of Applications and Proceedings in the Patent and Trademark Office

Applications filed in the Patent and Trademark Office and accepted as complete applications are assigned for examination to the respective examining groups having charge of the classes of inventions to which the applications relate. In the examining group applications are taken in the order in which they have been filed or in accordance with examining procedures established by the Commissioner.

The examination of the application consists of a study of the application for compliance with the legal requirements and a search through the prior art represented by prior United States patents, prior foreign patents which are available in the United States Patent and Trademark Office, and such prior literature as may be available, to see if the invention is new.

OFFICE ACTION

The applicant is notified in writing of the examiner's decision by an "action" which is mailed to the attorney or agent. The reasons for any adverse action or any objection or requirement are stated in the action, and such information or references are given as may be useful in aiding the applicant to decide whether or not to continue the prosecution of his application.

The examiner's action is complete as to all matters, except when there is a misjoinder of invention, fundamental defects in the application, or the like, in which case the action of the examiner may be limited to such matters before further action is made. However, matters of form need not be raised by the examiner until a claim is found allowable.

If the invention is not considered patentable, or not considered patentable as claimed, the claims, or those considered unpatentable, will be rejected. If the examiner finds that the invention as defined by the claims is not new, the claims are refused. The claims may also be refused if they differ somewhat from what is found to be old but the difference is not considered sufficient to justify a patent. It is not uncommon for some or all of the claims to be rejected on the first action by the examiner; relatively few applications are allowed as filed.

Terms such as "anticipation," "fully met," "lack of novelty," are used when rejecting claims under section 102 of the patent statute if the invention claimed is not new. Terms such as "unpatentable over" and "obvious over" are used when rejecting claims when the invention claimed is not sufficiently different from the prior art under section 103 of the patent statute to warrant a patent.

APPLICANT'S RESPONSE

After the Office action, if adverse in any respect, the applicant, if he wishes to persist in his application for a patent, must reply within the time allowed, and may request reexamination or reconsideration, with or without amendment.

In order to be entitled to reexamination or reconsideration, the applicant must make a request in writing, and he must distinctly and specifically point out the supposed errors in the examiner's action; the applicant must respond to every ground of objection and rejection in the prior Office action, and the applicant's action must appear throughout to be a bona fide attempt to advance the case to final action. The mere allegation that the examiner has erred will not be accepted as a proper reason for such reexamination or reconsideration.

In amending an application in response to a rejection, the applicant must clearly point out the patentable novelty which he thinks the claims present in light of the Office's objections.

After response by the applicant the application will be reexamined and reconsidered, and the applicant will be notified if claims are rejected, or objections or requirements made, in the same manner as after the first examination. The second Office action is usually final.

FINAL REJECTION

On the second or any subsequent examination or consideration, the rejection or other action may be made final, whereupon the applicant's response is limited to appeal in the case of rejection of any claim, and further amendment is restricted. A petition may be taken to the Commissioner in the case of objections or requirements not involved in the rejection of any claim. Response to a final rejection or action must include cancellation of, or appeal from the rejection of, each claim so rejected and, if any claim stands allowed, compliance with any requirement or objection as to form.

In making such final rejection, the examiner repeats or states all grounds of rejection then considered applicable to the claims in the case.

Interviews with examiners may be arranged, but an interview does not remove the necessity for response to Office actions within the required time, and the action of the Office is based solely on the written record.

If two or more inventions are claimed in a single application, and are regarded by the Patent and Trademark Office to be of such a nature that a single patent may not be issued for both of them, the applicant will be required to limit the application to but one of the inventions. The other invention may be made the subject of a separate application which, if filed while the first application is still pending, will be entitled to the benefit of the filing date of the first application. A requirement to restrict the application to one invention may be made before further action by the examiner.

On the average, two out of every three applications for patents are approved by the Patent and Trademark Office.

AMENDMENTS TO APPLICATION

The following are some further details concerning amendments to applications:

The applicant may amend before or after the first examination and action as specified in the rules, or when and as specifically required by the examiner.

After final rejection or action amendments may be made canceling claims or complying with any requirement of form which has been made, but the admission of any such amendment or its refusal, and any proceedings relative thereto, shall not operate to relieve the application from its condition as subject to appeal or save it from abandonment.

If amendments touching the merits of the application are presented after final rejection, or after appeal has been taken, or when such amendment might not otherwise be proper, they may be admitted upon a showing of good and sufficient reasons why they are necessary and were not earlier presented.

No amendment can be made as a matter of right in appealed cases. After decision on appeal, amendments can only be made as provided in the rules.

The specifications, claims, and drawing must be amended and revised, when required, to correct inaccuracies of description and definition of unnecessary words, and to secure correspondence between the claims, the description, and the drawing.

All amendments of the drawings or specifications, and all additions thereto, must conform to at least one of them as it was at the time of the filing of the application. Matter not found in either, involving a departure from or an addition to the original disclosure, cannot be added to the application even though supported by a supplemental oath or declaration, and can be shown or claimed only in a separate application.

The claims may be amended by canceling particular claims, by presenting new claims, or by amending the language of particular claims (such amended claims being in effect new claims). In presenting new or amended claims, the applicant must point out how they avoid any reference or ground of rejection of record which may be pertinent.

Erasures, additions, insertions, or alterations of the papers and records must not be made by the applicant. Amendments are made by filing a paper directing or requesting that specified changes or additions be made. The exact word or words to be stricken out or inserted in the application must be specified, and the precise point indicated where the deletion or insertion is to be made.

Amendments are "entered" by the Office by making the proposed deletions by drawing a line in red ink through the word or words canceled and by making the proposed substitutions or insertions in red ink, small insertions being written in at the designated place and larger insertions being indicated by reference.

No change in the drawing may be made except by permission of the Office. Permissible changes in the construction shown in any drawing may be made only by the Office. A sketch in permanent ink showing proposed changes, to become part of the record, must be filed. The paper requesting amendments to the drawing should be separate from other papers. The drawing may not be withdrawn from the Office.

Substitute drawings will not ordinarily be admitted in any case unless required by the Office.

If the number or nature of the amendments renders it difficult to consider the case, or to arrange the papers for printing or copying, the examiner may require the entire specification or claims, or any part thereof, to be rewritten. A substitute specification will ordinarily not be accepted unless it has been required by the examiner.

The original numbering of the claims must be preserved throughout the prosecution. When claims are canceled, the remaining claims must not be renumbered. When claims are added by amendment or substituted for canceled claims, they must be numbered by the applicant consecutively beginning with the number next following the highest numbered claim previously presented. When the application is ready for allowance, the examiner, if necessary, will renumber the claims consecutively in the order in which they appear or in such order as may have been requested by applicant.

TIME FOR RESPONSE AND ABANDONMENT

The response of an applicant to an action by the Office must be made within a prescribed time limit.

The maximum period for response is set at 6 months by the statute. The statute also provides that the Commissioner may shorten the time for reply to not less than 30 days. The usual period for response to an Office action is 3 months. Upon request, and for sufficient cause, a shortened time for reply may be extended up to the maximum 6 months period. If no reply is received within the time period, the application is considered as abandoned and no longer pending. However, if it can be shown that the failure to prosecute was unavoidable, the application may be revived by the Commissioner. This revival requires a petition to the Commissioner, accompanied by a verified showing of the cause of the delay and a fee for the petition, which should be filed without delay. The proper response must also accompany the petition if it has not yet been filed.

APPEAL TO THE BOARD OF APPEALS AND TO THE COURT

If the examiner persists in his rejection of any of the claims in an application, or if the rejection has been made final, the applicant may appeal to the Board of Appeals in the Patent and Trademark Office. The Board of Appeals consists of the Commissioner of Patents and Trademarks, the Assistant Commissioners, and not more than fifteen examiners-in-chief, but normally each appeal is heard by only three members. An appeal fee is required, and the applicant must file a brief to support his position. He is entitled to an oral hearing if he desires one.

As an alternative to appeal, in situations where an applicant desires consideration of different claims or further evidence, a new continuation application is often filed. The new application requires a filing fee and should submit the claims and evidence for which consideration is desired. If it is filed before expiration of the period for appeal and specific reference is made therein to the earlier application, the applicant will be entitled to his earlier filing date for subject matter common to both applications.

If the decision of the Board of Appeals is still adverse to the applicant, he has a choice of appealing to the Court of Customs and Patent Appeals or of filing a civil action against the Commissioner of Patents and Trademarks in the United States District Court for the District of Columbia. The court in the appeal will review the record made in the Patent and Trademark Office and may affirm or reverse the action taken by the Patent and Trademark Office. In the civil action, the applicant may present testimony in the court, and the court will make a decision holding that he either is or is not entitled to the patent.

INTERFERENCES

Occasionally two or more applications are filed by different inventors claiming substantially the same patentable invention. The patent can only be granted to one of them, and a proceeding known as an "interference" is instituted by the Patent and Trademark Office to determine who is the first inventor and entitled to the patent. About 1 percent of the applications filed become involved in an interference proceeding. Interference proceedings may also be instituted between an application and a patent already issued, provided the patent has not been issued for more than 1 year prior to the filing of the conflicting application, and provided that the conflicting application is not barred from being patentable for some other reason.

Each party to such a proceeding must submit evidence of facts proving when he made the invention. In view of the necessity of proving the various facts and circumstances concerning the making of the invention during an interference, inventors must be able to produce evidence to do this. If no evidence is submitted a party is restricted to the date of filing his application as his earliest date. The priority question is determined by a board of three interference examiners on the evidence submitted. From the decision of the Board of Patent Interferences, the losing party may appeal to the Court of Customs and Patent Appeals or file a civil action against the winning party in the appropriate United States district court.

The terms "conception of the invention" and "reduction to practice" are encountered in connection with priority questions. Conception of the invention refers to the completion of the devising of the means for accomplishing the result. Reduction to practice refers to the actual construction of the invention in physical form; in the case of a machine it includes the actual building of the machine, in the case of an article or composition it includes the actual making of the article or composition, in the case of a process it includes the actual carrying out of the steps of the process; and actual operation, demonstration, or testing for the intended use is also usually necessary. The filing of a regular application for patent completely disclosing the invention is treated as equivalent to reduction to practice. The inventor who proves to be the first to conceive the invention and the first to reduce it to practice will be held to be the prior inventor, but more complicated situations cannot be stated this simply.

Allowance and Issue of Patent

If, on examination of the application, or at a later stage during the reexamination or reconsideration of the application, the patent application is found to be allowable, a notice of allowance will be sent to the applicant, his attorney, or his agent.

The basic issue fee for each original or reissue patent, except in design cases, is $100. There is an additional fee of $10 for each page (or portion thereof) of the specification as printed, and $2 for each sheet or drawing.

The written notice of allowance is accompanied by an estimate of the issue fee determined in accordance with the number of pages in the specification and the number of sheets of drawing. This issue fee must be paid within three months from the date of the notice, and if it is not, the application is considered abandoned (forfeited).

The notice of any remaining balance of the issue fee is sent to the applicant at the time of the grant of the patent. If this remaining balance is not paid within three months therefrom the patent lapses.

A provision is made in the statute whereby the Commissioner may accept the fee up to 3 months late, on a showing of unavoidable delay. When the issue fee is paid, the patent issues as soon as possible after the date of payment, depending on the volume of printing on hand. The patent grant then is delivered or mailed on the day of its grant, or as soon thereafter as possible, to the inventor or to the inventor's attorney or agent if there is one on record.

On the date of the grant, the record of the patent in the Patent and Trademark Office becomes open to the public. Printed copies of the specification and drawing are available on that same date, or shortly thereafter.

In case the publication of an invention by the granting of a patent would be detrimental to the national defense, the patent law gives the Commissioner of Patents and Trademarks the power to withhold the grant of the patent and to order the invention kept secret for such period of time as the national interest requires.

Nature of Patent and Patent Rights

The patent is issued in the name of the United States under the seal of the Patent and Trademark Office, and is either signed by the Commissioner of Patents and Trademarks or has his name written thereon and attested by an official of the Patent and Trademark Office. The patent contains a grant to the patentee and a printed copy of the specification and drawing is annexed to the patent and forms a part of it. The grant to the pantentee is of "the right to exclude others from making, using or selling the invention throughout the United States" for the term of 17 years. The United States in this phrase includes territories and possessions.

The exact nature of the right conferred must be carefully distinguished, and the key is in the words "right to exclude" in the phrase just quoted. The patent does not grant the right to make, use, or sell the invention but only grants the exclusive nature of the right. Any person is ordinarily free to make, use, or sell anything he pleases, and a grant from the government is not necessary. The patent only grants the right to exclude others from making, using, or selling the invention. Since the patent does not grant the right to make, use, or sell the invention, the patentee's own right to do so is dependent upon the rights of others and whatever general laws might be applicable. A patentee, merely because he has received a patent for an invention, is not thereby authorized to make, use, or sell the invention if doing so would violate any law. An inventor of a new automobile would not be entitled to use his new automobile in violation of the laws of a state requiring a license, because he has obtained a patent, nor may a patentee sell an article when its sale is forbidden by a law, merely because he has obtained a patent. Neither may a patentee make, use, or sell his own invention if doing so would infringe upon the prior rights of others. A patentee may not violate the Federal antitrust laws or the pure food and drug laws, by virtue of his having a patent. Ordinarily there is nothing which prohibits a patentee from making, using, or selling his own invention, unless he thereby infringes anothers' patent which is still in force.

Since the essence of the right granted by a patent is the right to exclude others from commercial exploitation of the invention, the patentee is the only one who may make, use, or sell his invention. Others may not do so without authorization from the patentee. The patentee may manufacture and sell the invention himself, or he may license others to do so.

The term of a patent is 17 years. After the patent has expired anyone may make, use, or sell the invention without permission of the patentee, provided that matter covered by other unexpired patents is not used. The term may not be extended except by special act of Congress.

Correction of Patents

Once the patent is granted, it is outside the jurisdiction of the Patent and Trademark Office except in the following respects.

The Patent and Trademark Office may issue without charge a certificate correcting a clerical error it has made in the patent when the patent does not correspond to the record in the Patent and Trademark Office. These are mostly corrections of typographical errors made in printing.

Some minor errors of a typographical nature made by the applicant may be corrected by a certificate of correction for which a charge is made.

The patentee may disclaim one or more claims of his patent by filing in the Patent and Trademark Office a disclaimer as provided by the statute.

When the patent is defective in certain respects, the law provides that the patentee may apply for a reissue patent. This is a patent granted to replace the first one and is granted only for the balance of the unexpired term. However, the nature of the changes that can be made by means of the reissue are rather limited; new matter cannot be added.

Assignments and Licenses

A patent is personal property and may be sold to others or mortgaged; it may be bequeathed by a will, and it may pass to the heirs of a deceased patentee. The patent law provides for the transfer or sale of a patent, or of an application for patent, by an instrument in writing. Such an instrument is referred to as an assignment and may transfer the entire interest in the patent. The assignee, when the patent is assigned to him, becomes the owner of the patent, and he has the same rights that the original patentee had.

The statute also provides for the assignment of a part interest, that is, a half interest, a fourth interest, etc., in a patent. There may also be a grant which conveys the same character of interest as an assignment but only for a particularly specified part of the United States.

A mortgage of patent property passes ownership thereof to the mortgagee or lender until the mortgage has been satisfied and a retransfer from the mortgagee back to the mortgagor, the borrower, is made. A conditional assignment also passes ownership of the patent and is regarded as absolute until canceled by the parties or by the decree of a competent court.

An assignment, grant, or conveyance of any patent or application for patent should be acknowledged before a notary public or officer authorized to administer oaths or perform notarial acts. The certificate of such acknowledgment constitutes prima facie evidence of the execution of the assignment, grant, or conveyance.

RECORDING OF ASSIGNMENTS

The Patent and Trademark Office records assignments, grants, and similar instruments sent to it for recording, and the recording serves as notice. If an assignment, grant, or conveyance of a patent or an interest in a patent (or an application for patent) is not recorded in the Patent and Trademark Office within 3 months from its date, it is void against a subsequent purchaser for a valuable consideration without notice, unless it is recorded prior to the subsequent purchase.

An instrument relating to a patent should identify the patent by number and date (the name of the inventor and title of the invention as stated in the patent should also be given). An instrument relating to an application should identify the application by its serial number and date of filing, and the name of the inventor and title of the invention as stated in the application should also be given. Sometimes an assignment of an application is executed at the same time that the application is prepared and before it has been filed in the Patent and Trademark Office. Such assignment should adequately identify the application, as by its date of execution and name of the inventor and title of the invention, so that there can be no mistake as to the application intended.

If an application has been assigned and the assignment is recorded on or before the date the issue fee is paid, the patent will be issued to the assignee as owner. If the assignment is of a part interest only, the patent will be issued to the inventor and assignee as joint owners.

JOINT OWNERSHIP

Patents may be owned jointly by two or more persons as in the case of a patent granted to joint inventors, or in the case of the assignment of a part interest in a patent. Any joint owner of a patent, no matter how small his part interest, may make, use, and sell the invention for his own profit, without regard to the other owner, and may sell his interest or any part of it, or grant licenses to others, without regard to the other joint owner, unless the joint owners have made a contract governing their relation to each other. It is therefore dangerous to assign a part interest without a definite agreement between the parties as to the extent of their respective rights and their obligations to each other.

The owner of a patent may grant licenses to others.

Since the patentee has the right to exclude others from making, using, or selling the invention, no one else may do any of these things without his permission. A license is the permission granted by the patent owner to another to make, use, or sell the invention. No particular form of license is required; a license is a contract and may include whatever provisions the parties agree upon, including the payment of royalties, etc.

The drawing up of a license agreement (as well as assignments) is within the field of an attorney at law, although such attorney should be familiar with patent matters as well. A few states have prescribed certain formalities to be observed in connection with the sale of patent rights.

Infringement of Patents

Infringement of a patent consists in the unauthorized making, using, or selling of the patented invention within the territory of the United States, during the term of the patent. If a patent is infringed, the patentee may sue for relief in the appropriate Federal court. He may ask the court for an injunction to prevent the continuation of the infringement, and he may also ask the court for an award of damages because of the infringement. In such an infringement suit, the defendant may raise the question of the validity of the patent, which is then decided by the court. The defendant may also aver that what he is doing does not constitute infringement. Infringement is determined primarily by the language of the claims of the patent, and if what the defendant is making does not fall within the language of any of the claims of the patent, he does not infringe.

Suits for infringement of patents follow the rules of procedure of the Federal courts. From the decision of the district court, there is an appeal to the appropriate Federal court of appeals. The Supreme Court may thereafter take a case by writ of certiorari. If the United States government infringes a patent, the pantentee has a remedy for damages in the Court of Claims of the United States. The government may use any patented invention without permission of the patentee, but the patentee is entitled to obtain compensation for the use by or for the government.

If the patentee notifies anyone that he is infringing his patent or threatens suit, the one charged with infringement may himself start the suit in a Federal court and get a judgment on the matter.

The Patent and Trademark Office has no jurisdiction over questions relating to infringement of patents. In examining applications for patent no determination is made as to whether the invention sought to be patented infringes any prior patent. An improvement invention may be patentable, but it might infringe a prior unexpired patent for the invention improved upon, if there is one.

Patent Marking and "Patent Pending"

A patentee who makes or sells patented articles, or a person who does so under him, is required to mark the articles with the word "Patent" and the number of the patent. The penalty for failure to mark is that the patentee may not recover damages from an infringer unless the infringer was duly notified of the infringement and continued to infringe after the notice.

The marking of an article as patented when it is not in fact patented is against the law and subjects the offender to a penalty.

Some persons mark articles sold with the terms "Patent Applied For" or "Patent Pending." These phrases have no legal effect, but only state that an application for patent has been filed in the Patent and Trademark Office. The protection afforded by a patent does not start until the actual grant of the patent. False use of these phrases or their equivalent is prohibited by law.

Design Patents

The patent laws provide for the granting of design patents to any person who has invented any new, original, and ornamental design for an article of manufacture. The design patent protects only the appearance of an article, and not its structure or utilitarian features. The proceedings relating to granting of design patents are the same as those relating to other patents, with a few differences.

The filing fee on each design application is $20; the issue fee is $10 for a $3\frac{1}{2}$-year term, $20 for a 7-year term, and $30 for a 14-year term. If on examination an applicant is considered entitled to a design patent under the law, a notice of allowance will be sent to him, his attorney, or his agent, calling for the payment of an issue fee in an appropriate amount depending on the duration of term desired by the applicant.

The drawing of the design patent conforms to the same rules as other drawings, but no reference characters are required.

The specification of a design application is short

and ordinarily follows a set form (see p. 90). Only one claim is permitted per form.

Plant Patents

The law also provides for the granting of a patent to anyone who has invented or discovered and asexually reproduced any distinct and new variety of plant, including cultivated sports, mutants, hybrids, and newly-found seedlings, other than a tuber-propagated plant or a plant found in an uncultivated state.

Asexually propagated plants are those that are reproduced by means other than from seeds, such as by the rooting of cuttings, by layering, budding, grafting, inarching, etc.

With reference to tuber-propagated plants, for which a plant patent cannot be obtained, the term "tuber" is used in its narrow horticultural sense, meaning a short, thickened portion of an underground branch. The only plants covered by the term "tuber-propagated" are the Irish potato and the Jerusalem artichoke.

An application for a plant patent consists of the same parts as other applications.

The application papers for a plant patent and any responsive papers pursuant to the prosecution must be filed in duplicate, but only one need be signed (in the case of the application papers the original should also be signed); the second copy may be a legible carbon copy of the original. The duplicate file is then submitted to the Agricultural Research Service, Department of Agriculture, for an advisory report on the plant variety, the original file being retained in the Patent and Trademark Office at all times.

The specification should include a complete detailed description of the plant and the characteristics thereof that distinguish the same over related known varieties, and its antecedents, expressed in botanical terms in the general form followed in standard botanical textbooks or publications dealing with the varieties of the kind of plant involved (evergreen tree, dahlia plant, rose plant, apple tree, etc.), rather than a mere broad nonbotanical characterization such as commonly found in nursery or seed catalogs. The specification should also include the origin or parentage of the plant variety sought to be patented and must particularly point out where and in what manner the variety of plant has been asexually reproduced. Where color is a distinctive feature of the plant the color should be positively identified by reference to a designated color as given by a recognized color dictionary. Where the plant variety originated as a newly-found seedling, the specification must fully describe the conditions (cultivation, environment, etc.) under which the seedling was found growing to establish that it was not found in an uncultivated state.

A plant patent is granted on the entire plant. It therefore follows that only one claim is necessary and only one is permitted.

The oath or declaration required of the applicant, in addition to the statements required for other applications, must include the statement that the applicant has asexually reproduced the new plant variety.

Plant patent drawings are not mechanical drawings and should be artistically and competently executed. The drawing must disclose all the distinctive characteristics of the plant capable of visual representation. When color is a distinguishing characteristic of the new variety, the drawing must be in color. Two duplicate copies of color drawings must be submitted. Color drawings may be made either in permanent watercolor or oil, or in lieu thereof may be photographs made by color photography or properly colored on sensitized paper. The paper in any case must correspond in size, weight, and quality to the paper required for other drawings. Mounted photographs are acceptable.

Specimens of the plant variety, its flower or fruit, should not be submitted unless specifically called for by the examiner.

All inquiries relating to plant patents and pending plant patent applications should be directed to the Patent and Trademark Office and not to the Department of Agriculture.

The Plant Variety Protection Act (Public Law 91–577, approved December 24, 1970) provides for a system of protection for sexually reproduced varieties, for which protection was not previously provided, under the administration of a newly established

Plant Variety Protection Office within the Department of Agriculture. Requests for information regarding the protection of sexually reproduced varieties should be addressed to Commissioner, Plant Variety Protection Office, Consumer and Marketing Service, Grain Division, 6525 Bellcrest Road, Hyattsville, Maryland 20782.

Treaties and Foreign Patents

Since the rights granted by a United States patent extend only throughout the territory of the United States and have no effect in a foreign country, an inventor who wishes patent protection in other countries must apply for a patent in each of the other countries. Almost every country has its own patent law, and a person desiring a patent in a particular country must make an application for patent in that country, in accordance with their requirements.

The laws of many countries differ in various respects from the patent law of the United States and even from each other. In most foreign countries, publication of the invention before the date of the application will bar the right to a patent. In most foreign countries, a series of fees are due after the grant of the patent. These fees are usually annual and increase in amount each year. Most foreign countries require that the patented invention must be manufactured in that country after a certain period, usually 3 years. If there is no manufacture within this period, the patent may be void in some countries, although in most countries the patent may be subject to the grant of compulsory licenses to any other person who may apply for a license.

There is a treaty relating to patents which is adhered to by 79 countries, including the United States, and is known as the Paris Convention for the Protection of Industrial Property. It provides that each country guarantees to the citizens of the other countries the same rights in patent and trademark matters that it gives to its own citizens. The treaty also provides for the right of priority in the case of patents, trademarks, and industrial designs (design patents). This right means that, on the basis of a regular first application filed in one of the member countries, the applicant may, within a certain period of time, apply for protection in all the other member countries. These later applications will then be regarded as if they had been filed on the same day as the first application. Thus, these later applications will have priority over applications for the same invention which may have been filed during the said period of time by other persons. Moreover, these later applications, being based on the first application, will not be invalidated by any acts accomplished in the interval, such as, for example, publication or exploitation of the invention, the sale of copies of the design, or use of the trademark. The period of time mentioned above, within which the subsequent applications may be filed in the other countries, is 12 months in the case of applications for patent and 6 months in the case of industrial designs and trademarks.

Another treaty, known as the Patent Cooperation Treaty, was negotiated at a diplomatic conference in Washington, D.C., in June of 1970. It has been signed by 35 countries, including the United States. The treaty came into force on January 24, 1978. International applications could be filed as of June 1, 1978. The treaty facilitates the filing of applications for patent on the same invention in member countries by providing for, among other things, centralized filing procedures and a standardized application format.

A number of patent attorneys specialize in obtaining patents in foreign countries. In general, an inventor should be satisfied that he could make some profit from foreign patents or that there is some particular reason for obtaining them, before he attempts to apply for foreign patents.

Under United States law it is necessary, in the case of inventions made in the United States, to obtain a license from the Commissioner of Patents and Trademarks before applying for a patent in a foreign country. Such a license is required if the foreign application is to be filed before an application is filed in the United States or before the expiration of 6 months from the filing of an application in the United States. The request for a license may be a simple letter referring to the United States application if one has already been filed. After 6 months from the United States filing, a license is not required unless the invention has been ordered to be kept secret. If the invention has been ordered to be kept secret, consent to the filing abroad must be obtained from the Commissioner of Patents and Trademarks during the period in which the order of secrecy is in effect.

Foreign Applicants for United States Patents

The patent laws of the United States make no discrimination with respect to the citizenship of the inventor. Any inventor, regardless of his citizenship, may apply for a patent on the same basis as an American citizen. There are, however, a number of particular points of special interest to applicants located in foreign countries.

The application for patent in the United States must be made by the inventor, and the inventor must sign the papers (with certain exceptions), differing from the law in many countries where the signature of the inventor and an oath of inventorship are not necessary. If the inventor is dead, the application may be made by his executor or administrator, or equivalent, and in the case of mental disability it may be made by his legal representative (guardian).

No United States patent can be obtained if the invention was patented abroad before applying in the United States by the inventor or his legal representatives or assigns on an application filed more than 12 months before filing in the United States. Six months are allowed in the case of a design patent.

An application for patent filed in the United States by any person who has previously regularly filed an application for a patent for the same invention in a foreign country which affords similar privileges to citizens of the United States, has the same force and effect as if filed in the United States on the date the application was first filed in the foreign country, provided the application in the United States is filed within 12 months (6 months in the case of a design patent) from the earliest date on which any such foreign application was filed. A copy of the foreign application certified by the patent office of the country in which it was filed is required to secure this right of priority.

If any application for patent has been filed in any foreign country by the applicant or by his legal representatives or assigns prior to his application in the United States, the applicant must, in the oath or declaration accompanying the application, state the country in which the earliest such application has been filed, giving the date of filing the application; and all applications filed more than a year before the filing in the United States must also be cited in the oath or declaration.

An oath or declaration must be made with respect to every application. When the applicant is in a foreign country the oath or affirmation may be made before any diplomatic or consular officer of the United States, or before any officer having an official seal and authorized to administer oaths in the foreign country, whose authority shall be proved by a certificate of a diplomatic or consular officer of the United States, the oath being attested in all cases by the proper official seal of the officer before whom the oath is made.

When the oath is taken before an officer in the country foreign to the United States, all the application papers (except the drawing) must be attached together and a ribbon passed one or more times through all the sheets of the application, and the ends of the ribbons brought together under the seal before the latter is affixed and impressed, or each sheet must be impressed with the official seal of the officer before whom the oath was taken.

If the application is filed by the legal representative (executive, administrator, etc.) of a deceased inventor, the legal representative must make the oath or declaration.

When a declaration is used, the ribboning procedure is not necessary, nor is it necessary to appear before an official in connection with the making of a declaration.

A foreign applicant may be represented by any patent attorney or agent who is registered to practice before the United States Patent and Trademark Office.

List of Fees and Payment

The following fees and charges are payable to the Patent and Trademark Office:

1. Filing fee. On filing each application for an original patent, except in design cases $65.00

   In addition:

   On filing or on presentation at any other time, for each claims in independent form which is in excess of one 10.00

   For each claim (whether independent or dependent) which is in excess of 10 .... 2.00

   Errors in payment of the additional fees may be rectified in accordance with regulations of the Commissioner.

2. Issue fee. For issuing each original or reissue patent, except in design cases ... 100.00

   In addition:

   For each page (or portion thereof) of specification as printed 10.00

   For each sheet of drawing 2.00

3. In design cases:
   a. On filing each design application $20.00
   b. On issuing each design patent:
      For 3 years and 6 months 10.00
      For 7 years 20.00
      For 14 years 30.00
4. Reissues. On filing each application for
   the reissue of patent 65.00
   In addition:
   On filing or on presentation at any
      other time, for each claim in inde-
      pendent form which is in excess of
      the number of independent claims
      of the original patent 10.00
   For each claim (whether independent
      or dependent) which is in excess of
      ten and also in excess of the number
      of claims of the original patent 2.00
   Errors in payment of the additional fees
      may be rectified in accordance with
      regulations of the Commissioner.
5. On filing each disclaimer 15.00
6. On filing each petition for the revival of
   an abandoned application for patent .   15.00
7. On filing each petition for the delayed
   payment of the issue fee 15.00
8. On appeal for the first time from the examiner to the Board of Appeals 15.00
   On filing a brief in support of the ap-
      peal 50.00
9. For certification of copies of records, etc.,
   in any case, in addition to the cast of
   copy certified 1.00
10. For certificate of correction of applicant's
    mistake 15.00
11. For uncertified copies of the specifica-

tions and accompanying drawings of
patents, except design patents ...... .50

12. For uncertified copies of design patents . .20

13. For recording every assignment, agreement, or other paper relating to the
property in a patent or application .. 20.00
For additional item, where the document
relates to more than one patent or
application 3.00

14. For typewritten copies of records, for
each page produced (double-spaced)
or fraction thereof 1.50

15. For photocopies or other reproductions
of records, drawings or printed material, per page of material copied ...... .30

16. For abstracts of title to catch patent or
application:
For the search, one hour or less, and certificate 3.00
Each additional hour or fraction thereof 1.50
For each brief from the digest of assignments, of 200 words or less 1.00
Each additional 100 words or fraction
thereof .... .10

17. For translations from foreign languages
into English, made only of references
cited in applications or of papers filed
in the Patent and Trademark Office
insofar as facilities may be available:
Written translations, for every 100 words
of the original language, or fraction
thereof 5.00
Oral translations (dictation or assis-
tance), for each one-half hour or fraction thereof that service is rendered . 4.00

18. For making patent drawings, when facil-

ities are available, the cost of making the same, minimum charge per sheet .	25.00
19. For correcting drawings, the cost of making the correction, minimum charge .	3.00
20. For the mounting of unmounted drawings and photoprints received with patent applications, provided they are of approved permanency	2.00
21. Lists of U.S. Patents:	
All patents in a subclass, per sheet (containing 100 patent numbers or less)	.50
Minimum charge per order	1.00
Patents in a subclass limited by date or patent number, per sheet (containing 50 numbers or less)	.50
Minimum charge per order	1.00
22. Search of Patent and Trademark Office records for purposes not otherwise specified in this section, per one-half hour of search or fraction thereof ...	$3.00
23. For special service to expedite furnishing items or services ahead of regular order:	
On orders for copies of U.S. patents and trademark registrations, in addition to the charge for the copies, for each copy ordered	.50
On all other orders or requests for which special service facilities are available, in addition to the regular charge, a special service charge equal to the amount of regular charge; minimum special service charge per order or request	1.00

24. For air mail delivery:

 On 'special service' orders to destinations to which U.S. domestic air mail postage rates apply, no additional charge.

 On regular service orders to any destination and "special service" orders to destination other than those specified in the preceding subparagraph, an additional charge equal to the amount of air mail postage. (Available only when the ordering party has, with the Patent and Trademark Office, a deposit account.)

25. For items and services, that the Commissioner finds may be supplied, for which fees are not specified by statute or by this section, such charge as may be determined by the Commissioner with respect to each such item or service.

26. International application filing and processing fees.

 a. The following fees and charges are established by the Patent and Trademark Office under the authority of 35 U.S.C. 376:

   1. A transmittal fee (see 35 U.S.C. 361(d) and PCT Rule 14) .... $ 35.00

   2. A search fee (see 35 U.S.C. 361(d) and PCT Rule 16) $300.00

   3. A supplemental search fee when required (see PCT Art. 17(3)(a) and PCT Rule 40.2)—per additional invention $200.00

4. The national fee, that is, the amount set forth as the filing fee under 35 U.S.C. 41(a)(1).
   5. A special fee when required (see 35 U.S.C. 372(c)—per claim .... $ 10.00
b. The basic fee and designation fee portions of the international fee shall be as prescribed in PCT Rule 15.

The following microfilm lists are sold by the U.S. Department of Commerce, National Technical Information Service, Springfield, Va. 22151, to whom all communications respecting the same should be addressed:

Microfilm Lists of Patents. The reels containing the mechanical, electrical, and chemical patent numbers in original and cross-referenced classification may be purchased for $70.00 or individual reels for $6.00 per reel (identified as PB 185–900). The classification of all design patents is listed on a single reel which may be purchased for $6.00 (PB 185–917).

The following publications are sold, and the prices for them fixed, by the Superintendent of Documents, Government Printing Office, Washington, D.C. 20402, to whom all communications respecting the same should be addressed:

Official Gazette of the United States Patent Office:
         Annual subscription, domestic $342.20
         Annual subscription, foreign 427.75
         Single numbers 6.60
   Annual Index Relating to Patents, price varies.
   Manual of Classifications of Patents 44.00
         Foreign 55.00

THE ABOVE PRICES ARE SUBJECT
TO CHANGE WITHOUT NOTICE.

All payment of money required for Patent and Trademark Office fees should be made in United States specie, treasury notes, national bank notes, post office money orders or postal notes payable to the Commissioner of Patents and Trademarks, or by certified checks. If sent in any other form, the Office may delay or cancel the credit until collection is made. Postage stamps are not acceptable. Money orders and checks must be made payable to the Commissioner of Patents and Trademarks. Remittances from foreign countries must be payable and immediately negotiable in the United States for the full amount of the fee required.

Money paid by actual mistake or in excess, such as payment not required by law, will be refunded, but a mere change of purpose after the payment of money, as when a person desires to withdraw his application for a patent or to withdraw an appeal, will not entitle him to demand such a return. Amounts of 50 cents or less will not be returned unless specifically demanded, nor will the payer be notified of such amount; amounts over 50 cents but less than $1 may be returned in postage stamps; and amounts of $1 or more will be refunded by check.

Sample Forms

The following forms illustrate how to prepare parts of applications for patent and other papers (see p. 28, under "application for patent" for size of paper and preferred writing). Forms for patent specifications and drawings are not given since these vary so considerably. Specifications and drawings of patents may be inspected and studied in those libraries which maintain collections of patents (see p. 22). Particular patents of interest can be located from the *Official Gazette* (see p. 14) and copies purchased.

1. PATENT APPLICATION, SOLE INVENTOR; POWER OF ATTORNEY, OATH

To the Commissioner of Patents and Trademarks:

Your petitioner, ..., a citizen of the United States and a resident of . . . ., State of . . . ., whose post-office address is . . . ., prays that letters patent may be granted to him for the improvement in . . . ., set forth in the following specification; and he hereby appoints . . . ., of . . . ., (Registration No. . . . .), his attorney (or agent) to prosecute this application and to transact all business in the Patent and Trademark Office connected therewith. (If no power of attorney is to be included in the application, omit the appointment of the attorney.)

[The specification, which includes the description of the invention and the claims, is written here.]

. . . ., the above-named petitioner, being sworn (or affirmed), deposes and says that he is a citizen of the United States and resident of . . . ., State of . . . ., that he verily believes himself to be the original, first and sole inventor of the improvement in . . . . described and claimed in the foregoing specification; that he does not know and does not believe that the same was ever known or used before his invention thereof, or patented or described in any printed publication in any country before his invention thereof, or more than one year prior to this application, or in public use or on sale in the United States more than one year prior to this application; that said invention has not been patented or made the subject of an inventor's certificate in any country foreign to the United States on an application filed by him or his legal representatives or assigns more than twelve months prior to this application; that he acknowledges his duty to disclose information of which he is aware which is material to the examination of this application; and that no application for patent or inventor's certificate on said invention has been filed by him or his representatives or assigns in any country foreign to the United States, except as follows: ....

....
(Inventor's full signature)

STATE OF .... ⎫
County of .... ⎭ ss:

Sworn to and subscribed before me
this .... day of ...., 19...

....
(Signature of notary or officer)

[SEAL]

....
(Official Character)

2. PATENT APPLICATION, JOINT INVENTORS; POWER OF ATTORNEY, OATH

To the Commissioner of Patents and Trademarks:

Your petitioners, ... and ...., citizens of the United States and residents, respectively, of ...., State of ...., and of ...., State of .... whose post-office addresses are, respectively, ... and .... pray that letters patent may be granted to them, as joint inventors, for the improvements in ...., set forth in the following specifications; and they hereby appoint ...., of .... (Registration No ....), their attorney (or agent), to prosecute this application and to transact all business in the Patent and Trademark Office connected therewith. (If no power of attorney is to be included in the application, omit the appointment of the attorney.)

[The specification, which includes the description of the invention and the claims, is written here.]

.... and ...., the above-named petitioners, being sworn (or affirmed), depose and say that they are citizens of the United States and residents of ...., State of ...., that they verily believe themselves to be the original, first and joint inventors of the improvement in .... described and claimed in the foregoing specification; that they do not know and do not believe that the same was ever known or used before their invention thereof, or patented or described in any printed publication in any country before their invention thereof, or more than one year prior to this application, or in public use or on sale in the United States for more than one year prior to this application; that said invention has not been patented or made the subject of an inventor's certificate in any country foreign to the United States on an application filed by them or their legal representatives or assigns more than 12 months prior to this application; that they acknowledge their duty to disclose information of which they are aware which is material to the examination of this application, and that no application for patent or inventor's certificate on said invention has been filed by them or their representatives or assigns in any country foreign to the United States, except as follows: ....

....
(Inventor's full signature)

STATE OF .... }
County of .... } ss:

Sworn to and subscribed before me
this .... day of ...., 19...

....
(Signature of notary or officer)

[SEAL]

....
(Official character)

3. PATENT APPLICATION, ADMINISTRATOR OF ESTATE OF DECEASED INVENTOR; POWER OF ATTORNEY, OATH

To the Commissioner of Patents and Trademarks:

Your petitioner, A .... B ...., a citizen of the United States and a resident of ...., State of ...., whose post-office address is ...., administrator of the estate of C .... D ...., late a citizen of the United States and a resident of ...., State of ...., deceased (as by reference to the duly certified copy of letters of administration, hereto annexed, will more fully appear), prays that letters patent may be granted to him for the invention of the said C .... D .... for an improvement in .... set forth in the following specification; and he hereby appoints ...., of .... (Registration No. ....), his attorney (or agent), to prosecute this application and to transact all business in the Patent and Trademark Office connected therewith.

(If no power of attorney is to be included in the application, omit the appointment of the attorney.)

[The specification, which includes the description of the invention and the claims, is written here.]

A .... B ...., the above-named petitioner, being sworn (or affirmed), deposes and says that he is a citizen of the United States of America and a resident of ...., that he is the administrator of the estate (or executor of the last will and testament) of C .... D ...., deceased, late a citizen of the United States and resident of ...., that he verily believes the said C .... D .... to be the original,

first and sole inventor of the improvement in
.... described and claimed in the foregoing
specification; that he does not know and does not believe
that the same was ever known or used before the invention
thereof by the said C .... D ....,
or patented or described in any printed publication in any
country before the said invention thereof, or more than
one year prior to this application, or in public use or on sale
in the United States for more than one year prior to this
application; that said invention has not been patented or
made the subject of an inventor's certificate in any country
foreign to the United States on an application filed by the
said C .... D .... or his legal
representatives or assigns more than 12 months prior to
this application; that he acknowledges his duty to disclose
information of which he is aware which is material to the
examination of this application, and that no application for
patent or inventor's certificate on said invention has been
filed by the said C .... D ....
or his representatives or assigns in any country foreign to
the United States, except as follows: ....

A .... B ....
(Signature)
ADMINISTRATOR, ETC.

STATE OF ....
County of .... } ss:

Sworn to and subscribed before me this
.... day of ...., 19...

[SEAL]

....
(Signature of notary or officer)

....
(Official character)

4. OATH NOT ACCOMPANYING APPLICATION

STATE OF . . . . ⎫
County of . . . . ⎬ *ss:*

. . . ., being sworn (or affirmed), deposes and says that he is a citizen of the United States of America and resident of . . . ., that on . . . ., 19. . ., he filed application for patent Serial No. . . . . in the United States Patent and Trademark Office, that he verily believes himself to be the original, first and sole inventor of the improvement in . . . . described and claimed in the specification of said application for patent; that he does not know and does not believe that the same was ever known or used before his invention thereof, or patented or described in any printed publication in any country before his invention thereof, or more than one year prior to the date of said application, or in public use or on sale in the United States for more than one year prior to the date of said application; that said invention has not been patented or made the subject of an inventor's certificate before the date of said application in any country foreign to the United States on an application filed by him or his legal representatives or assigns more than twelve months prior to the date of said application; that he acknowledges his duty to disclose information of which he is aware which is material to the examination of this application, and that no application for patent or inventor's certificate on said invention has been filed by him or his representatives or assigns in any country foreign to the United States, except as follows: ....

....
(Inventor's full signature)

Sworn to and subscribed before me
this .... day of ...., 19...,

....
(Signature of notary or officer)

[SEAL]

....
(Official character)

5. DESIGN APPLICATION, SPECIFICATION, OATH

To the Commissioner of Patents and Trademarks:

Your petitioner, ..., a citizen of the United States and a resident of .... in the county of .... and State of ...., whose post-office address is ...., city of ...., State of..., prays that letters patent may be granted him for the new and original design for ...., set forth in the following specification; and he hereby appoints ...., of ...., (Registration No. ....), his attorney (or agents), to prosecute this application and to transact all business in the Patent and Trademark Office connected therewith.

Be it known that I have invented a new, original, and ornamental design for .... of which the following is a specification, reference being had to the accompanying drawing, forming a part hereof.

The figure is a plan view of a ...., showing my new design.

I claim:

The ornamental design for a ...., as shown. ...., the above-named petitioner being sworm (or affirmed), deposes and says that he is a citizen of the United States and resident of county of ...., State of ...., that he verily believes himself to be the original, first, and sole inventor of the design for .... described and claimed in the foregoing specification; that he does not

know and does not believe that the same was ever known or used before his invention thereof, or patented or described in any printed publication in any country before his invention thereof, or more than one year prior to this application, or in public use or on sale in the United States for more than one year prior to this application; that said design has not been patented or made the subject of an inventor's certificate in any country foreign to the United States on an application filed by him or his legal representatives or assigns more than 6 months prior to this application; that he acknowledges his duty to disclose information of which he is aware which is material to the examination of this application, and that no application for patent or inventor's certificate on said design has been filed by him or his representatives or assigns in any country foreign to the United States, except as follows: ....
....

....
(Inventor's full signature)

State of   .... ⎫
County of   .... ⎬   *ss:*
                   ⎭

Sworn to and subscribed before me
this   .... day of   ...., 19...

[SEAL]

....
(Signature of notary or officer)

....
(Official character)

6. PLANT PATENT APPLICATION; POWER OF ATTORNEY, OATH

To the Commissioner of Patents and Trademarks:

Your petitioner, ..., a citizen of the United States and a resident of ...., in the State of ...., whose post-office address is ...., prays that letters patent may be granted to him for the new and distinct variety of ...., set forth in the following specification; and he hereby appoints .... of .... (Registration No. ....), his attorney (or agent), to prosecute this application and to transact all business in the Patent and Trademark Office connected therewith.

(If no power of attorney is to be included in the application, omit the appointment of the attorney.)

[The specification, which includes the description of the invention and the claims, is written here.]

........................, the above-named petitioner, being sworn (or affirmed), deposes and says that he is a citizen of the United States of America and resident of ...., that he verily believes himself to be the original, first, and sole inventor of the new and distinct variety of .... described and claimed in the foregoing specification; that he has asexually reproduced the said new and distinct variety; that he does not know and does not believe that the same was ever known or used before his invention thereof, or patented or described in any printed publication in any country before his invention thereof, or more than one year prior to this application, or in public use or on sale in the United States for more than one year prior to this application; that said invention has not been patented or made the subject of an inventor's certificate in any country foreign to the United States on an application filed by him or his legal representatives or assigns more than 12 months prior to this application; that he acknowledges his duty to disclose information of which he is aware which is material to the examination of this application, and that no application for patent or inventor's certificate on said new and distinct variety of plant has been filed by him or his representatives or assigns in any country foreign to the United States, except as follows: ....

....
(Inventor's full signature)

STATE OF .... ⎫
County of .... ⎭ ss:

Sworn to and subscribed before me
this .... day of ...., 19...,

....
(Signature of notary or officer)

[SEAL]

....
(Official character)

7. POWER OF ATTORNEY OR AUTHORIZATION OF AGENT, NOT ACCOMPANYING APPLICATION

To the Commissioner of Patents and Trademarks:

The undersigned having, on or about the ....
day of ...., 19..., made application for letters patent
for an improvement in ...., Serial Number ......,
hereby appoints .... of ....,
State of ...., Registration No. ....,
his attorney (or agent), to prosecute said application, and to
transact all business in the Patent and Trademark Office
connected therewith.

....
(Signature)

8. REVOCATION OF POWER OF ATTORNEY OR AUTHORIZATION OF AGENT

To the Commissioner of Patents and Trademarks:

The undersigned having, on or about the .... day of ...., 19..., appointed ...., of ...., State of ...., his attorney (or agent) to prosecute an application for letters patent which application was filed on or about the .... day of ...., 19..., for an improvement in ...., Serial Number ...., hereby revokes the power of attorney (or authorization of agent) then given.

....
(Signature)

9. ASSIGNMENT OF PATENT

(No special form is prescribed for assignments, which may contain various provisions depending upon the agreement of the parties. The following two forms are specimens of assignments which have been used in some cases.)

WHEREAS, I, ..., of ...., did obtain Letters Patent of the United States for an improvement in .... No. ...., dated ....; and whereas, I am now the sole owner of said patent; and,

WHEREAS, ..., of ...., whose post-office address is ...., City of ...., and State of ...., is desirous of acquiring the entire interest in the same;

Now, THEREFORE, in consideration of the sum of .... dollars ($ ....), the receipt of which is hereby acknowledged, and other good and valuable considerations, I, ..., by these presents do sell, assign, and transfer unto the said ...., the entire right, title, and interest in and to the said Letters Patent aforesaid; the same to be held and enjoyed by the said ...., for his own use and behoof, and for his legal representatives and assigns, to the full end of the term for which said Letters Patent are granted, as fully and entirely as the same would have been held by me had this assignment and sale not been made.

EXECUTED, this .... day of ...., 19..., at ....

STATE ....
County of .... } ss:

Before me personally appeared said ....
and acknowledged the foregoing instruments to be his free act and deed this .... day of ....,

....
(Notary Public)

[SEAL]

10. ASSIGNMENT OF APPLICATION

WHEREAS, I, ..., of ....
have invented certain new and useful Improvements in ..
..........................., for which an application
for United States Letters Patent was filed on
..................., Serial No. ....,
[if the application has been prepared but not yet filed, state
"for which an application for United States Letters Patent
was executed on ....," instead] and

WHEREAS, ..., of ....,
whose post-off address is ....,
is desirous of acquiring the entire right, title and interest in
the same;

Now, THEREFORE, in consideration of the sum of ....
.... dollars ($ ....),
the receipt whereof is hereby acknowledged, and other
good and valuable considerations, I, the said
..........................., by these presents do sell,
assign and transfer unto said ....,
the full and exclusive right to the said invention in the
United States and the entire right, title, and interest in and
to any and all Letters Patent which may be granted, therefore in the United States.

I hereby authorize and request the Commissioner of Patents and Trademarks to issue said Letters Patent to said ...., as the assignee of the entire right, title, and interest in and to the same, for his sole use and behoof; and for the use and behoof of his legal representatives, to the full end of the term for which said Letters Patent may be granted, as fully and entirely as the same would have been held by me had this assignment and sale not been made.

Executed this .... day of ...., 19..., at ....
....

State of ....
County of .... } *ss:*

Before me personally appeared said ....
and acknowledged the foregoing instrument to be his free act and deed this .... day of ...., 19...

....
(Notary Public)

[SEAL]

11. DECLARATION WHICH MAY BE INCLUDED IN AN APPLICATION IN LIEU OF AN OATH

(Rules 65 and 68 of the Rules of Practice provide for a declaration in lieu of an oath in certain instances. The petition and specification preceded the declaration.)

.........................., the above-named petitioner
.... declares that he is a citizen of the United States and resident of ....
that he verily believes himself to be the original, first, and sole inventor of the improvement in ....
described and claimed in the annexed specification; that he does not know and does not believe that the same was ever known or used before .... invention thereof, or patented or described in any printed publication in any country before his invention thereof, or more than one year prior to this application, or in public use or on sale in the United States more than one year prior to this application; that said invention has not been patented in any country foreign to the United States on an application filed by him or his legal representatives or assigns more than twelve months prior to this application; that he acknowledge his duty to disclose information of which he is aware

is material to the examination of this application, and that no application for patent on said invention has been filed by him or his representatives or assigns in any country foreign to the United States, except as follows:

. . . .

The undersigned petitioner . . . . declare . . . . further that all statements made herein of . . . . own knowledge are true and that all statements made on information and belief are believed to be true; and further that these statements were made with the knowledge that willful false statements and the like so made are punishable by fine or imprisonment, or both, under section 1001 of Title 18 of the United States Code and that such willful false statements may jeopardize the validity of the application or any patent issuing thereon.

Inventor's full name or names . . . .

. . . .
(Signature)

Date . . . .

PART TWO **TRADEMARKS**

Trademarks

In general, the laws governing trademarks are similar to those governing patents. The basic difference between patents and trademarks lies in their functions. While a patent protects an inventor from another person's passing the invention off as his own or illegally earning money from it, a trademark is simply a registered identification of goods or services. It does not give the owner of the mark exclusive rights over the product or service, but merely prevents anyone else from using the mark in commerce.

There is a distinction between trademarks per se, and service marks, certification marks, and collective marks. A trademark, as defined in the Trademark Act of 1946, "includes any word, name, symbol, or device used by a manufacturer or merchant to identify his goods and distinguish them from those manufactured or sold by others." A "service mark" is a mark used in sales or advertising to identify the services of one person and distinguish them from the services of others. Titles, character names, and other distinctive features of radio or television programs, for example, may be registered as service marks. A "certification mark" is a mark used by one or more persons other that the owner of the mark to certify the regional origin, material, mode of manufacture, quality, etc., of goods or services, or to certify that the work on these goods or services was performed by members of a union or other organization. A "collective mark" is a mark used by the members of a cooperative, association, or other collective group, including unions. All of these kinds of marks may be registered under the Trademark Act.

Use in commerce is required for the registration of any trademark. The mark must be displayed on a product, its package, or an accompanying label, or it must be displayed in the sale or advertising of a service. A trademark need not be registered in order for it to be used in commerce. It must, however, be registered if the user of the mark wishes to be regarded as its legal owner with exclusive rights of use. The mark must also clearly indicate that it is registered in order for the user to have full legal protection.

There are two registers in which a trademark may be registered, the Primary Register and the Supplemental Register. If a trademark is ineligible for the Primary Register, but has been in lawful use in commerce for the year preceding the filing of the application for registration, it may be registered on the Supplemental Register. Registration on the Supplemental Register does not give the right to prevent importation of goods bearing an infringing mark, but it does provide some protection to the owner by giving the right to sue in the United States Court.

Ordinarily, a trademark may not be registered if it

merely describes goods or services or their geographical location, or if it consists primarily of a surname. However, if an applicant can prove that a mark has been in substantially exclusive and continuous use in commerce for 5 years preceding the application date, the mark may be registered in the Primary Register.

Once the mark is registered, the words "Registered in the U.S. Patent and Trademark Office" or the letter R enclosed in a circle is used with it.

The application for registration of a trademark must be written in English, and it must include a drawing of the mark (on 8" $\times$ 11" white paper in India ink), 5 specimens or facsimiles (no larger than $8\frac{1}{2}$" $\times$ 13"), and a $35.00 fee for registration in each class. There are 42 official classifications of goods and services, and applications must indicate the one or more that apply to the mark. For a list of official classifications, as well as other detailed requirements concerning the presentation and form of applications, and a complete schedule of fees, the Office of Patents and Trademarks, Washington, D.C. 20231, should be consulted.

The process of examination of applications is similar to that of patents. The trademark division of the Patent and Trademark Office, like the patent division, has a Search Room in which a digest of registered marks is maintained, arranged according to classifications. The Search Room is open to the public, and it is advisable to check this digest before adopting a trademark to avoid possible conflict with previously registered marks.

Also like the Patent Office, the Trademark Office has several publications (including a section on trademarks in the *Official Gazette of the Patent Office*, which may be purchased or subscribed to separately) and furnishes copies of registrations for a fee.

Trademark registration lasts for 20 years and is renewable for another 20 years for an additional fee. But, in the sixth year after the registration of a mark, a declaration of use must be filed. This declaration must show that the mark is still in use, or that if it is not, nonuse is not intended as complete abandonment of its use. The same rule applies to renewal.

PART
THREE **COPYRIGHTS**

Copyrights

Federal copyright law lies within the same branch of federal law as patent and trademark law. A summary of copyright law is included in this book, because, like patent and trademark law, its purpose is to protect the work of individuals from fraud and piracy.

Basically, copyright applies to the form and manner of expression rather than to content. A news article, for example, could be copyrighted, but this would not give its author exclusive rights over the information contained in the article. It means that, in general, the article could not be reproduced, or read or displayed in public, without permission of the author.

Anything that is an original work may be copyrighted. The work does not have to be particularly new to the public. It only has to be something that the author made, and did not copy from something else. One could not, for example, copyright an exact replica of a sculpture, but one could copyright a sculpture that bears many similarities to a pre-existing work. The originality can be minimal—the Copyright Office is not a judge of artistic merit. Written words, visual art, dramatic works, clothing and jewelry design, and much more can be copyrighted. The only requirement other than originality is that the work be in a fixed form of some kind, such as on paper, tape, film, canvas, or in solid form.

Copyright gives an author exclusive rights to use of the work itself. If someone writes a novel and owns copyright on it, he has the right to demand royalties from anyone who wants to reproduce it, or to deny permission to reproduce it altogether. But when a copyright legally expires, the work enters the public domain, that is to say, anyone can use the work for profit without risk of infringement on the rights of the author or his estate.

Copyright is a broad term. A work need not necessarily be registered with the Copyright Office to be copyrighted, but registration must be made in order for the full protection of the law to be assured. It behooves an author to apply for registered copyright on a finished piece for many reasons, not the least of which is for protection in the event of a lawsuit. If an author believes his registered work to have been illegally used, the law states that a court has the right to order such use to stop, to order the offender to pay the author for damages, to turn over to the author all profits from the illegal use, and to reimburse him for his legal fees in the lawsuit, within reason (the definition of which is at the court's discretion).

A greatly expanded and revised set of copyright laws went into effect on January 1, 1978. Very minimal changes had been made since 1909, and in the intervening 69 years many new methods of reproduction and communication had been developed. The new laws attempt to cover all of these. But perhaps most important is the change in the duration of copyright. Under the old law, the initial period of copyright was 28 years from the date on which copyright was secured, with the option of a single 28-year renewal, a total of 56 years. Under the new law, works in their renewal period before 1978 have the renewal time extended to 47 years, a total of 75 years. Works that have copyright renewed after 1978 also get a 47-year period of renewal. Copyright initially secure in 1978 or after lasts until 50 years after the author's death. In the case of anonymous or pseudonymous works, or works on which the copyright is owned by an employer rather than by their creator, the duration is 75 years from publication or 100 years from creation, whichever period ends first.

There is a clause in copyright law that entitles the public to "fair use" of part of a copyrighted work. This extends, in general, only to small excerpts from a work. One can publish a piece that includes a few lines quoted from a copyrighted story, giving credit to the author, without getting permission from the author, in most cases. The best rule to follow is to consult the specific copyright laws, available at many libraries, which give more detailed guidelines regarding fair use. One should be warned, however, that the description of fair use is deliberately vague in the law. This is to prevent rampant use of whole sections, or even more, without proper permission.

Libraries have special rights in reproducing copyrighted material. They can, in many circumstances, reproduce entire works for the private use of individuals. It is best to consult librarians in these cases, for they are familiar with the intricacies of copyright law. Other circumstances under which special rights sometimes apply are educational and charitable uses.

Copyright law requires that a user obtain a license from the Copyright Office for recording copyrighted musical works, playing recordings in jukeboxes, and using certain kinds of copyrighted material in noncommercial broadcasts and cable television. In these cases, the user must pay a fee to the Copyright Office, and the author or owner of the copyright can then collect a percentage of this fee by placing a claim with the Copyright Royalty Tribunal.

In order to secure a registered copyright, an author must file an application with the Copyright Office which includes a $10.00 fee, to: Register of Copyrights, Library of Congress, Washington, D.C. 20559. In most cases, it is also necessary to deposit two copies of the work with the Office (this is for the Library of Congress). Once copyright is secured, the work must carry an official notice of copyright. It is best to get the specific instructions for the proper notice directly from the Copyright Office for each copyrighted work, because a notice with errors or omissions could result in forfeiting of copyright. Copyright can, of course, be legally transferred. This must be done through the Copyright Office.

NOTES

NOTES

NOTES

NOTES